TIME WORD PROBLEMS

W9-BYK-874

Lisa Colozza Cocca

Crabtree Publishing Company
www.crabtreebooks.com

Author: Lisa Colozza Cocca
Publishing plan research and development:
   Sean Charlebois, Reagan Miller
   Crabtree Publishing Company
Editors: Crystal Sikkens, Ruth Frederick, Leslie Jenkins, Phyllis Jelinek
Proofreaders: Kelly McNiven, Lisa Slone
Editorial director: Kathy Middleton
Production coordinator: Shivi Sharma
Creative director: Amir Abbasi
Cover design: Margaret Amy Salter
Photo research: Nivisha Sinha
Production coordinator and prepress technician: Margaret Amy Salter
Print coordinators: Katherine Berti, Margaret Amy Salter

Photographs:

Cover: Shutterstock; Page 1: AlexSmith/Shutterstock; Page 4: Ana Abejon / iStockphoto.com (l); Page 4: Nicole S. Young / iStockphoto.com (c); Page 4: drbimages / iStockphoto.com (r); Page 4: Kelvin Wong / Shutterstock.com (b); Page 7: Nicole S. Young / iStockphoto.com (l); Page 7: Africa Studio / Shutterstock.com (l); Page 7: Mark Bowden / iStockphoto.com (r); Page 9: Ana Abejon / iStockphoto.com (l); Page 9: Nicole S. Young / iStockphoto.com (c); Page 9: drbimages / iStockphoto.com (r); Page 10: Photonot Stop RM / IndiaPicture; Page 12: Rob Wilson / Shutterstock.com; Page 14: Africa Studio / Shutterstock.com; Page 16: Noah Strycker / Shutterstock.com; Page 18: Marcell Mizik / Shutterstock.com; Page 20: iofoto / Shutterstock.com.

Artwork Created by Planman technologies: Pages 5; 6; 13.

(t = top, b = bottom, l = left, c= center, r = right)

Library and Archives Canada Cataloguing in Publication

Cocca, Lisa Colozza, 1957-
   Time word problems / Lisa Colozza Cocca.

(My path to math)
Includes index.
Issued in print and electronic formats.
ISBN 978-0-7787-1077-6 (bound).--ISBN 978-0-7787-1093-6 (pbk.).--
ISBN 978-1-4271-9273-8 (pdf).--ISBN 978-1-4271-9197-7 (html)

   1. Time measurements--Juvenile literature. 2. Word problems
(Mathematics)--Juvenile literature. I. Title. II. Series: My path to math

QB209.5.C633 2013   j529'.7   C2013-902664-9
                                     C2013-902665-7

Library of Congress Cataloging-in-Publication Data

CIP available at Library of Congress

Crabtree Publishing Company

Printed in the USA/052013/JA20130412

www.crabtreebooks.com   1-800-387-7650

Published in Canada
Crabtree Publishing
616 Welland Ave.
St. Catharines, ON
L2M 5V6

Published in the United States
Crabtree Publishing
PMB 59051
350 Fifth Avenue, 59th Floor
New York, New York 10118

Published in the United Kingdom
Crabtree Publishing
Maritime House
Basin Road North, Hove
BN41 1WR

Published in Australia
Crabtree Publishing
3 Charles Street
Coburg North
VIC, 3058

Contents

Clocks, Clocks, and More Clocks

Piper and Malcolm are visiting Mr. Tucker's clock shop. The shop has many kinds of clocks. Piper points out the clock she likes best. Mr. Tucker says it is an **analog clock**.

Analog clocks have the numbers 1 through 12 around the **face**. They have an hour hand, a minute hand, and a second hand. The hands move around the face in a circle. The hands show the time.

This is an analog clock. The shorter hand points to the hour. The longer hand points to the minutes. The red hand counts the seconds.

Malcolm shows Piper another clock. Mr. Tucker says it is a **digital clock**. It only uses numbers to show the time. The hours are on the left side of the **colon (:)**. The minutes are on the right side of the colon (:).

This is a digital clock.

Activity Box

Match the clocks that tell the same time.

Parts of a Day: a.m. and p.m.

The analog clock only has enough numbers to count 12 hours, but Piper knows there are 24 hours in a day. Mr. Tucker shows Malcolm and Piper a chart. It shows all 24 hours. After 12, the numbers start at 1 again.

12:00 a.m. – midnight
1:00 a.m.
2:00 a.m.
3:00 a.m.
4:00 a.m.
5:00 a.m.
6:00 a.m.
7:00 a.m.
8:00 a.m.
9:00 a.m.
10:00 a.m.
11:00 a.m.
12:00 p.m. – noon
1:00 p.m.
2:00 p.m.
3:00 p.m.
4:00 p.m.
5:00 p.m.
6:00 p.m.
7:00 p.m.
8:00 p.m.
9:00 p.m.
10:00 p.m.
11:00 p.m.

The time for each day is broken into two parts. Each part has 12 hours, and each hour is given a number. Hour number 12 that comes in the middle of the day is called **noon**. Hour number 12 that comes in the night is called **midnight**. We call the time from midnight until noon **a.m.** We call the time from noon to midnight **p.m.**

Mr. Tucker asks the children to name something they do every day. Malcolm eats breakfast at 7 a.m. He can use eating breakfast to remember what a.m. means. Piper gets ready for bed at 8 p.m. That can help her remember what p.m. means.

Activity Box

Is it a.m. or p.m.?

I go to school at 8 _____.

I eat supper at 6 _____.

Time Word Problems

On Saturday the clock store opens at 10 a.m. It closes at 5 p.m. Mr. Tucker asks Malcolm and Piper to find out how many hours in total the store is open that day.

Piper thinks this sounds like a word problem. She decides to break the problem into steps. Mr. Tucker helps the children write the steps.

Time Word Problems

1. What does the problem ask you to do? Look for clue words. Check to see if the times are a.m. or p.m.

2. How will you solve the problem? Will you add or subtract?

3. Use a clock, a number line, or a number sentence to help you.

4. Do the math.

5. Does your answer make sense?

Malcolm and Piper make a list of clue words to help them solve word problems.

Addition (+)	Subtraction (−)
in all	how many left
altogether	how many more
in total	how many less
later	how many fewer
time will be	earlier
longer	before
	time was

Using a Number Line to Measure Time

Piper sees the clue words "in total." She knows they need to **add** to solve the problem. Malcolm sees that the problem will be tricky. The store opens in the a.m. hours and closes in the p.m. hours. Mr. Tucker thinks a **number line** will help the children figure out the answer.

> ### Word Problem #1
> A store opens at 10 a.m. It closes at 5 p.m. How many hours in total is the store open?

CLOCKS FOR SALE: FIND THE TIME HERE!

10

Piper draws the number line. She starts at the left at 10 a.m. Then she makes a mark for each hour until 5 p.m. She labels the line 10 a.m., 11 a.m., 12 p.m., and when she reaches 12, she starts again with 1.

Next the children count the hours. They start at 10 a.m. They are adding, so they go from left to right as they count. They stop counting at the 5 p.m. mark. The store is open for 7 hours each day.

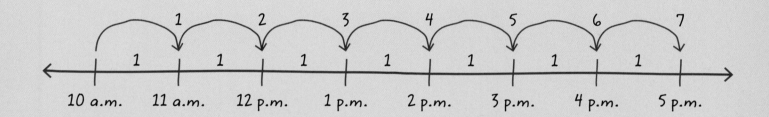

Activity Box

Malcolm goes to school from 8 a.m. to 3 p.m. How many hours in total does he go to school each day? Make a number line to help you solve the problem.

Counting Time by 5s

Do you see the clue words in the problem? They are "will it be." These words tell the children they need to add. Mr. Tucker says they will add in groups of five minutes. Malcolm says he can count by 5s. Mr. Tucker says counting time by 5s is different from counting objects. He draws a clock.

Word Problem #2

It is now 10:50 a.m. A delivery truck will bring some new clocks to the store in 25 minutes. What time will it be when the truck arrives at the store?

Mr. Tucker draws an analog clock and then he writes numbers around the clock. He writes the numbers by 5-minute intervals: 5, 10, 15, 20, 25, 30, 35, 40, 45, 50, and 55. After 55, Mr. Tucker writes 0. There are 60 minutes in 1 hour. When we read time, 1:55 is 1 hour and 55 minutes. When we reach 60 minutes, we add an hour and start the minutes back to 0. So, 5 minutes after 1:55 is 2:00. Ten minutes after 1:55 is 2:05.

The children use the clock Mr. Tucker has drawn. They start counting at 10:50. They count to 25 by 5s.

The delivery truck will be at the store at 11:15 a.m.

Activity Box

The school bus comes at 7:15 a.m. It will be 15 minutes late today. What time will the bus come? Use the clock to help you count by 5s.

13

Using a Number Line to Learn the Time

Mr. Tucker gives Piper and Malcolm another problem. Malcolm sees the clue words "will it be." The children know that these words tell them that they should add to solve this problem. They will count by 5s again. This time they will use a number line.

Word Problem #3

At 12:45 p.m., I ordered a pizza. It will take 20 minutes for the pizza to get here. What time will it be then?

14

Piper draws the number line. She makes 1 mark for every 5 minutes. Malcolm and Piper start counting at 12:45. They count to 20 by 5s from left to right. What time will the pizza get there? That's right! The pizza will be there at 1:05 p.m.

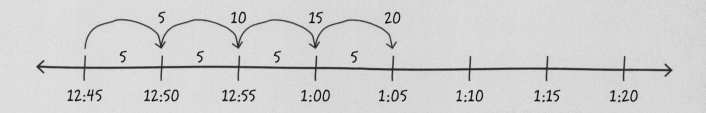

Activity Box

Mrs. Tucker decides to bake a pizza. The pizza goes in the oven at 12:20 p.m. It will cook for 25 minutes. What time will the pizza be ready? Make a number line to help you solve the problem.

Using a Number Line to Subtract Time

Piper sees the clue words "how many more" in the next word problem. To solve this problem,

Word Problem #4

Piper and Malcolm left their homes at the same time. Malcolm got to the clock store at 9:12 a.m. Piper got there at 9:20 a.m. How many more minutes did it take Piper to get to the store?

Malcolm and Piper need to **subtract**. When they needed to add, they counted from the left on a number line. To subtract, they will start on the right.

Malcolm draws the number line. Each mark stands for 1 minute. Malcolm and Piper start at 9:20. They count by 1s from right to left. It took Piper 8 minutes longer than Malcolm to get to the store.

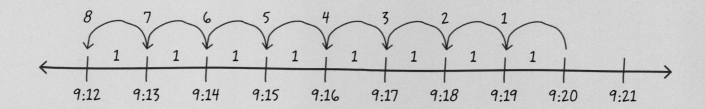

Activity Box

Mr. Lee and Ms. Abdullah come to the store at 2:05 p.m. Mr. Lee leaves at 2:13 p.m. Ms. Abdullah leaves at 2:21 p.m. How many more minutes did Ms. Abdullah spend in the store than Mr. Lee? Make a number line to help you solve the problem.

There's More Than One Way to Solve a Problem!

Mr. Tucker gives Malcolm and Piper another problem to solve. Do you see the clue words?

Malcolm draws a number line. He starts with 1 hour, 45 minutes. He makes a mark for every 5 minutes. He ends at 2 hours, 20 minutes. Malcolm will subtract. He starts on 2 hours, 20 minutes. He moves left as he counts by 5s. Using the number line, he sees that it took 35 fewer minutes to fix Clock B.

Word Problem #5

Mr. Tucker fixed two clocks. Clock A took 2 hours and 20 minutes to fix. Clock B took 1 hour and 45 minutes to fix. How many fewer minutes did it take Mr. Tucker to fix Clock B than Clock A?

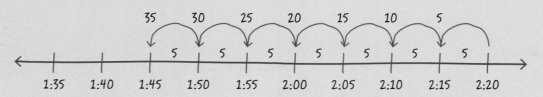

Mr. Tucker says there is often more than one way to solve a problem. He shows Piper how to use a number sentence. The words "how many fewer" mean she will subtract.

> 2 hours, 20 minutes
> – 1 hour, 45 minutes
> _____
> ?

There are two different units of time involved— hours and minutes.

Mr. Tucker tells Piper she must start with the minutes. Piper knows that 45 is greater than 20. She will have to borrow some minutes from one of the hours to subtract. Piper remembers that one hour is the same as 60 minutes.

> 2 hours, 20 minutes = 1 hour, (60 minutes + 20 minutes)
>   = 1 hour, 80 minutes

Now she is ready to subtract.

> $\overset{7}{\cancel{1}}$ hour, $\overset{10}{\cancel{80}}$ minutes
> – 1 hour, 45 minutes
> _____
> 0 hours, 35 minutes

Activity Box

On Monday, Piper jumps rope for 1 hour. On Tuesday, she jumps rope for 42 minutes. How many more minutes did Piper jump rope on Monday than on Tuesday? Show two ways to solve the problem.

Write Your Own Word Problem

The children write a word problem for Mr. Tucker to solve.

Word Problem #6

Piper and Malcolm each wrote a story. They started writing at the same time. Malcolm finished at 3:55 p.m. Piper wrote for 25 minutes longer than Malcolm. What time did Piper finish writing her story?

Mr. Tucker sees the clue word "longer." He will add. He draws a number line starting at 3:55. Each mark stands for 5 minutes. He moves to the right, counting to 25 by 5s. He stops at 4:20 p.m.

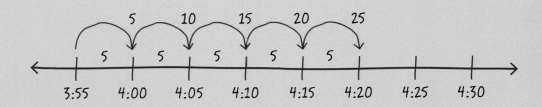

Mr. Tucker writes a number sentence.

> **3 hours, 55 minutes + 25 minutes = ?**
> **or   3:55 + 0:25 = ?**

Then he adds them together.

> **3:55**
> **+ 0:25**
> _____
> **3:80**

Mr. Tucker knows that 80 minutes is greater than one hour. He takes 60 minutes, which is also 1 hour, away from 80 minutes to find how many minutes are left over.

> **80 – 60 = 20 minutes**

He then adds the 1 hour to the hour group.

> **3 + 1 = 4 hours**

Mr. Tucker shows that Piper finished writing her story at 4:20 p.m.

Activity Box

Write your own word problem. Remember to use clue words. Then solve your problem with a number sentence.

Glossary

a.m. The hours between midnight and noon, sometimes written AM

add Join or combine two or more numbers or things together to make a new total or sum

analog clock A tool used to measure time; it uses movable hour, minute, and second hands to show the time in numbers from 1 through 12

colon (:) A punctuation mark used to separate the hours and minutes in time, the hours are on the left of the mark, the minutes are on the right of the mark

digital clock A tool used to measure time; the time is shown in numbers, and there are no movable hands on a digital clock

face [of a clock] The front; the side marked with numbers

midnight The name given to 12 o'clock in the middle of the night; 12 a.m.

noon The name given to 12 o'clock in the middle of the day; 12 p.m.

number line A line with numbers placed in the correct order

p.m. The hours between noon and midnight, sometimes written PM

subtract Take one number away from another

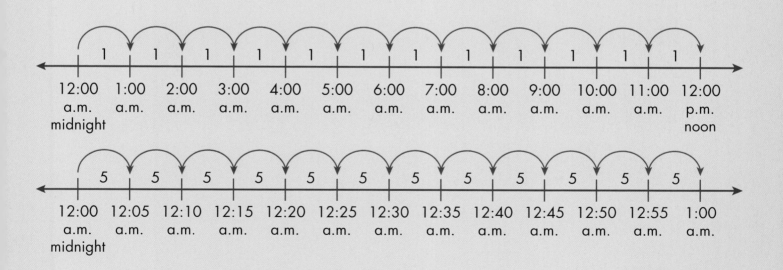

Index

Learning More

Stop the Clock

The site allows students to drag and drop items to match analog clocks and digital time. Children can play multiple times to try to better their time.

http://resources.oswego.org/games/stoptheclock/sthec3.html

That Quiz: Math Time

The site offers multiple quizzes on time. Users can choose between reading the time, adding time, subtracting time, and regrouping minutes to hours or hours to minutes. Children can time themselves as they answer the questions.

www.thatquiz.org/tq-g/math/time/

Beginner Word Problems
(My Path to Math) Minta Berry; Crabtree Publishing, 2012.

This book introduces the basics of solving word problems.

Time (My Path to Math) Penny Dowdy; Crabtree Publishing, 2009.

This book introduces the basics of telling time.